British Wild Flowers

Written and photographed by Harry Stanton

Ladybird Books Loughborough

January - February onwards

Garden Location

Snowdrop

Snowdrops are one of the first wild flowers to appear each year, even when the ground may be covered in snow. They grow in damp woods and are often planted in gardens. This plant was probably brought to Britain from Europe in medieval times.

Height 5 to 15 cm
Flowering January to April
Flower size 20 to 25 mm

Groundsel

Groundsel is a common weed found almost everywhere in Britain. The plant can be eaten by rabbits and birds but is poisonous to humans.

Height 15 to 50 cm
Flowering January to
December
Flower size 3 to 5 mm

Shepherd's Purse

This common weed of garden and wasteland is easily recognised by its heart-shaped seed pods. This shape is said to look like an old form of purse often used by country people and this is how the plant got its name.

Height 10 to 90 cm
Flowering January to
December
Other name: Pickpocket
Flower size 2 to 3 mm

5

Violets

There are many kinds of violets, but only the sweet violet has a scent. They grow on banks, under hedges and in woods.

Violets are found all over the British Isles but are only truly wild in the South and East of England.

Height 5 to 15 cm
Flowering February to June
Flower size 10 to 15 mm

Chickweed

This weak stemmed plant is very common in gardens, waste ground, pastures and woods. Because it flowers throughout the autumn, its seeds provide food for the birds.

Height 8 to 10 cm
Flowering February to
November
Flower size 8 to 10 mm

March onwards

Hedgerow

Lesser Celandine

The Lesser Celandine is not related to the Greater Celandine. The Lesser Celandine belongs to the same family as the buttercup and has a star-shaped flower. It is found in damp and shady places throughout the country.

Height 5 to 15 cm
Flowering March to May
Flower size 20 to 25 mm

Wood Anemone

One of the earliest spring flowers, these flowers grow in woods and meadows and always seem to be moving in the wind. The name Anemone comes from the

Greek word *anemos*, meaning wind.

Height 10 to 25 cm
Flowering March to May
Other name: Windflower
Flower size 25 to 35 mm

Primrose

One of the most common flowers in the woods, hedgerows and grassy places. Primroses are not often found near to towns because too many have been picked or dug up. It is found mostly in the western half of the British Isles and particularly likes clay soils.

Height 10 to 20 cm
Flowering March to May
Flower size 20 to 30mm

Butter Bur

Butter Bur has very large leaves often up to 1 metre in diameter which are very

hairy and white underneath. It grows on river banks and in damp places where the soil is sandy.
Since the flowers are rich in nectar, it is a favourite flower with bee keepers.

Height 15 to 30 cm
Flowering March to May
Flower size 2 to 3 mm

9

Marsh Marigold

This flower is very common beside streams, in marshy places and ditches. The flowers should not be picked for not only will they fade quickly, but the plant is poisonous.

Height 30 to 40 cm
Flowering March to June
Other names: Mollyblobs
                         Kingcup
In Scotland the
                    Lucken Gowan
           or Water Gowland
Flower size 10 to 50 mm

Lady's Smock

Another plant which grows in moist meadows and swampy places throughout Britain. The flowers close at night and when it rains. Its other name 'Cuckoo Flower' refers to the fact that it comes into bloom when the Cuckoo arrives, and disappears when it stops singing in June or July.

Height 15 to 35 cm
Flowering March to June
Other names: Cuckoo Flower
                         or Milk-maids
Flower size 12 to 20 mm

10

Germander Speedwell

A hairy-stemmed plant which grows along the ground on grassy hedge-banks. The long stems creep along the ground and send down roots before growing new plants.

There are eighteen different varieties of Speedwell growing in the British Isles.

Height 15 to 30 cm
Flowering March to July
Other names: Bird's Eye
*   Cat's Eye*
Break your Mother's Heart
Flower size 9 to 20 mm

Ground Ivy

This plant grows along the ground in woods, fields, grassy banks and beside hedges, fences and walls. One of its alternative names, Ale-hoof, reminds us that at one time the plant was

used in brewing beer. Beds of Ground Ivy have been known to live for over a hundred years.

Height 15 to 45 cm
Flowering March to June
Other names: Ale-hoof
*   Tun-hoof*
Flower size 8 to 12 mm

11

Daisy

This is perhaps the most common of all wild plants. The flowers turn towards the sun and close up at night and in dull weather. It gets its name from the original 'day's eye', because

of its reaction to changes in the amount of light.

Height 3 to 10 cm
Flowering March to October
Flower size 10 to 20 mm

Thrift

Thrift grows on the rocks and cliffs of the seashore or on high mountains. It has a long, thick, woody root, which enables it to survive in dry, stony, conditions.

It thrives even when constantly showered with salt sea spray.

Height 20 to 40 cm
Flowering March to October
Other name: Sea Pink
Flower size 18 to 25mm

Dandelion

Dandelions have very deep roots. The flowers close up at night and in dull weather. After fertilisation, each seed develops a 'parachute' and all together these form a fluffy ball on top of the

stem which is often called a Dandelion Clock. The seeds are then spread by the wind.

Height 15 to 30 cm
Flowering March to October
Flower size 35 to 50 mm

13

April onwards

Pasture

Cowslip

Cowslips grow in meadows and grassy places. The flowers have a sweet scent and the leaves are wrinkled and strongly veined on the

underside. It is rare in Scotland.
A wine made from the flowers was once thought to cure sleeplessness.

Height 5 to 15 cm
Flowering April to May
Other name: Paigle
Flower size 10 to 15 mm

Bluebell

Bluebells usually grow in shady woods and under hedges. In Scotland, the bluebell is known as the Wild Hyacinth. The 'Bluebells of Scotland' are known as Harebells in England.

Height 30 to 50 cm
Flowering April to May
Other names: Wild Hyacinth
Blue Bonnets
Pride of the Wood
Wood Bells
Flower sizes 10 to 20 mm

14

Jack by the Hedge

A very leafy plant the leaves of which smell of garlic when rubbed. The plant grows beside roads, hedges and in fields. The seed pods

are long and thin and in June the caterpillar of the Orange-Tip butterfly, which looks like the pods, can be found eating them.

Height 30 to 100 cm
Flowering April to June
Other name: Garlic Mustard
Flower size 8 to 10 mm

Ramsons

Ramsons grow close together in damp woodlands and on roadsides. When the leaves are broken or rubbed they smell of onions or garlic.

Height 20 to 30 cm
Flowering April to June
Other name: Wild Garlic
Flower size 10 to 20 mm

15

Stitchwort

Stitchwort is found in open hedges, bushy places and woods. The thin straggling stems rely on other plants for support. It gets its name from the old belief that it cured the pain in the side called "stitch".

Height 15 to 30 cm
Flowering April to June
Other name: Adder's Meat
Flower size 20 to 30 mm

Wild Strawberry

This plant has a woody stem clothed in silky hairs.
It grows over shady banks and around woods. The hairy leaves are oblong with edges cut into coarse teeth.

The fruit is much smaller but sweeter than the large garden variety.

Height 5 to 20 cm
Flowering April to July
Flower size 12 to 18 mm

Red Dead Nettle

Both Red Dead Nettle and White Dead Nettle have hollow square stems. Stinging Nettles have solid round stems.

Height 15 to 30 cm
Flowering April to August
Flower size 10 to 15 mm

Vetch

A climbing plant with slightly hairy stems which grows in fields, beside roads and on waste land.
There are five species which grow wild in the British Isles: Narrow-leaved Vetch, Common Vetch, Tufted Vetch, Wood Vetch and Bush Vetch.

Height 15 to 90 cm
Flowering April to September
Other names: Fitches
Twaddgers
Flower size 10 to 30 mm

17

Red Campion

Red Campion grows in moist shady places, woods and hedgerows. The flowers open in the daytime and close at night.

Height 30 to 60 cm
Flowering April to October
Other names: Robin's Eye
*   Bob Robin*
*   Rob in the*
*   Hedge*
Flower size 15 to 25 mm

White Dead Nettle

Although the leaves of the White Dead Nettle are very similar to the Stinging Nettle the plants are not related and it does not sting.

Height 30 to 60 cm
Flowering April to August
Flower size 20 to 25 mm

Buttercup

There are many kinds of Buttercup. They vary considerably in size and in the way they grow. The commonest is probably the Meadow Buttercup, but the Creeping Buttercup is often more noticeable because it

produces runners and spreads very rapidly. They are not eaten by animals because they have a bitter taste and are poisonous.

Height 15 to 100 cm
Flowering April to October
Other name: Bulbous
*   Crowfoot*
Flower sizes 10 to 20 mm

Stinging Nettle

The stems and leaves are covered with stinging hairs which break off when touched, causing irritation to the skin. The plant was used by the Romans to cure rheumatism.

Height 60 to 150 cm
Flowering April to October

19

Greater Plantain

Gardeners do not like Plantains because they grow in grassy places such as lawns with the leaves so close to the ground that they do not get cut when the grass is mown. The flowers grow on tall stalks.

Height 15 to 60 cm
Flowering April to September
Other names: White Man's
Foot
Rat's Tails
Cock Grass

Dock

There are many kinds of Dock. All except the Blood-veined variety, which has dark crimson veins, have entirely green leaves. Some varieties have broad leaves and some have narrow or curly leaves.

The leaves of the Broad Dock, when crushed and rubbed on the skin, are supposed to lessen the pain caused by the hairs on Stinging Nettles.

Height 30 to 100 cm
Flowering April to October
Other name: Dockens

21

May onwards

Water Meadow

Cuckoo Pint

Cuckoo Pint is found under hedges and in woodlands. The berries are poisonous. The pale green hood called a spathe folds over to hide the flowers beneath the purple spike.

Height 15 to 50 cm
Flowering May to June
Other names: Lords and
Ladies
Jack in the
Pulpit
Wake-robin
Wild Arum
Cuckoo Pintle

Comfrey

This common hairy plant grows in ditches, and wet shady places. The flowers vary in colour from creamy white to purple. It is often used by farmers and gardeners as a form of "green manure"

Height 60 to 120 cm
Flowering May to July
Flower sizes 5 to 10 mm

23

Yellow Flag

Beside streams, ponds and marshes Yellow Flags can be found throughout Britain. The leaves are stiff and have hard sharp edges which can cut you if you try to pick them.

Height 60 to 120 cm
Flowering May to August
Other name: Yellow Iris
Flower size 80 to 100 mm

Hemlock

Hemlock is a very poisonous plant and is recognised by its smooth hollow purple spotted stem and a strong unpleasant smell. It is common in ditches, damp waste land and on the banks of streams.

Height 100 to 200 cm
Flowering May to August
Flower size 3 to 4 mm

Sorrel

Sorrel is found in grassy places and open spaces in woods. The flowering stem has leaves which cling to it. The leaves do not have stalks.
The leaves have a strong taste and can be used for flavouring food.

Height 50 to 80 cm
Flowering May to August

Thistles

There are many members of the Thistle family. All of them have prickly leaves, and some have prickly stems. They grow in hedgesides or on waste ground and spread very easily because of the fine thistledown which can be carried for several kilometres on the wind.

Height 30 to 180 cm
Flowering May to September
Flower size 10 to 50 mm

Foxglove

Foxgloves are found in dry wastelands in woods and hedges. It is a poisonous plant. They are normally fertilised by humble bees, whose hairy bodies collect the pollen and carry it from flower to flower.

A valuable drug, digitalis, is extracted from the Foxglove plant and used in the treatment of heart disease.

Height 30 to 150 cm
Flowering May to September
Other names: Fairy Thimble
Deadman's
Bells
Flower size 20 to 30 mm

Forget-me-not

There are several kinds of Forget-me-nots. Most grow in damp, shady places and often grow in water.

The flowers change from pink to blue as they open. Sometimes the plant is called Scorpion Grass because the flower head looks like a scorpion's tail before the flowers open.

Height 15 to 50 cm
Flowering May to September
Other name: Scorpion Grass
Flower size 6 to 10 mm

Heartsease

Heartsease or Wild Pansy are flowers which vary in colour from yellow to violet. They are found on waste ground and in grassy places.

Height 10 to 20 cm
Flowering May to September
Flower size 10 to 25 mm

Red Clover

In grassy fields and on roadsides Red Clover can be found. It is a valuable food crop for cattle and sheep and at one time the dried flowers were used as a cough cure. It provides a large supply of nectar for bees which pollinate it.

Height 10 to 30 cm
Flowering May to October
Other name: Bee Bread
Flower size 20 to 40 mm

Scarlet Pimpernel

These flowers close in bad weather and at the approach of rain. They are found in gardens, fields and beside roads and are used by

country folk as a cheap barometer. Since the flowers tend to close anyway in the early afternoon, it is only effective in this way during the morning.

Height 15 to 30 cm
Flowering May to September
Other name: Poor Man's
*   Weather Glass*
Flower size 8 to 10 mm

Watercress

Watercress is a salad plant which grows in shallow streams and ditches. The plant will not grow in water which becomes polluted by farms, factories or

chemicals. Its thick hollow stem floats on the water and roots grow down from this.

Height 15 to 30 cm
Flowering May to October
Flower size 5 to 10 mm

Herb Robert

Very common in hedgebanks, woods and stony places. The pink flowers droop in bad weather and at night. It is easily recognised by its finely divided leaves often tinged with red and its strong, unpleasant smell.
This herb is thought to be named after Robert, Duke of Normandy, a medieval doctor.

Height 15 to 30 cm
Flowering May to October
Flower size 15 to 20 mm

June onwards

Pasture

Field Poppy

The Poppy has very hairy stems and leaves. One pair of petals is always larger than the others. Oil is extracted from the seeds of the Poppy and is used in cooking and in the preparation of artists' oil paints, but the juice of the plant is poisonous.

Other names: Corn Rose
Corn Poppy
Red Cap

Height 30 to 60 cm
Flowering June to August

Flower size 70 to 100 mm

Ox-Eye Daisy

Ox-Eye Daisies grow on sunny banks, especially where the soil is poor, and in hayfields and pastureland. The white petals are arranged in layers, rather like the tiles on a roof.

Height 30 to 60 cm
Flowering June to August
Other names: Marguerite
*   Dog Daisy*
In Scotland: Horse Gowan
*   Moon Daisy*
Flower size 25 to 50 mm

Deadly Nightshade

This is a bush plant. It is rare and is very poisonous. The berries are black and look like cherries, but just one berry can kill.

It has large, dull, green leaves which have an unpleasant smell.

Height 100 to 200 cm
Flowering June to August
Other names: Bella Donna
*   Dwale*
Flower size 25 to 30 mm

31

White Clover

White Clover can often be found in lawns and sports-fields as well as fields and roadsides. The leaves usually have three leaflets, but occasionally have four which is thought to be a

lucky charm. Different kinds of clover are grown by farmers, and many of these can be found growing wild.

Height 10 to 40 cm
Flowering June to August
Other names: Dutch Clover
Kentish Clover
Flower size 15 to 30 mm

Feverfew

This plant was once used by herbalists to cure people of fever. The leaves have a pleasant scent, and the plant

is found on waste land and grassy banks.

Height 30 to 60 cm
Flowering June to September
Flower size 10 to 15 mm

Meadow Sweet

This sweet scented plant is found in damp fields and ditches, wet meadows and by streams or rivers and is therefore a common flower in the fen country. The flowers produce no nectar but the sweet smell attracts insects which pollinate the plant.

Height 60 to 120 cm
Flowering June to September
Other name: Queen of the
*   Meadows*
Flower sizes 2 to 5 mm

Hogweed

A very common plant with flower heads up to 20 cm across. It grows by roadsides, fields and in woods, and has a thick, grooved, hairy stem. It is one of a large family known as *Umbelliferae*,

meaning umbrella-like. The flowers are carried on stems arranged like the ribs of an umbrella.

Height 60 to 200 cm
Flowering June to September
Other names: Keck
*   Cow Parsnip*
Flower sizes 3 to 4 mm

Purple Loosestrife

Purple Loosestrife grows in marshy places and riversides. It has a deep root from which new stems

grow each year. The lance shaped leaves have no stalk and clasp the stem just beneath the flowers.

Height 50 to 160 cm
Flowering June to September
Flower size 10 to 15 mm

Yellow Mignonette

This plant usually grows on dry, chalky soil. Although superficially similar to the Sweet Mignonette that is grown in gardens, the wild version lacks the delicate scent of the cultivated form.

Height 30 to 60 cm
Flowering June to September
Flower size 5 to 6 mm

Honeysuckle

Honeysuckle climbs over hedges and other plants. The flowers have a sweet scent, which becomes

stronger in the evening. Because the flowers are rich in nectar, they are great favourites with many insects.

Height 100 to 700 cm
Flowering June to September
Other name: Woodbine
Flower size 30 to 50 mm

Lesser Bindweed

Lesser Bindweed is a much smaller plant than Greater Bindweed and the almond-scented flowers last only for one day. The scent and nectar are particularly attractive to long-tongued insects which can reach into the funnel-shaped flower.

Height 10 to 60 cm
Flowering June to September
Other name: Field Bindweed
Flower size 30 to 50 mm

Woody Nightshade

Woody Nightshade is a poisonous plant and can be found in woods and hedges. It also spreads over pebbles on the seashore. The plant bears small, oval, red berries which can make you sick if swallowed. In the past, the *stems* were used to make medicines for treating rheumatism and skin complaints.

Height 50 to 200 cm
Flowering June to September
Other name: Bittersweet
Flower size 8 to 15 mm

Field Scabious

Field Scabious grows in dry grassy places. It was at one time known as the Scabies Herb and its juice was supposed to cure various sores and skin infections.

Height 30 to 100 cm
Flowering June to September
Other names: Clogweed
Gypsy Rose
Bachelor's Buttons
Lady's Cushion
Flower size 30 to 40 mm

37

Meadow Cranesbill

Often seen growing on green banks alongside roads and in meadows.

The Meadow Cranesbill is one of the most beautiful summer flowers and is a member of the geranium family.

Height 60 to 100 cm
Flowering June to September
Other names: Blue Basins
Blue Buttons
Granny's Bonnets
Loving Andrews
Flower size 25 to 30 mm

Knapweed

This tough-stalked plant is found in meadows and beside roads. It is seldom eaten by cattle because of its tough, wiry stem. This makes it an annoying weed in cultivated grassland.

Height 30 to 60 cm
Flowering June to September
Other names: Hard Heads
Knopweed
Drumstick
Flower size 10 to 50 mm

White Campion

White Campion has soft, hairy leaves and grows in fields, hedges and on wasteland. The flowers are open at night and attract night-flying moths. Because both White and Red Campion have separate male and female flowers, they often interbreed when growing close together and produce pink hybrids.

Height 30 to 90 cm
Flowering June to September
Flower sizes 15 to 25 mm

Birdsfoot Trefoil

Birdsfoot Trefoil gets its name from the shape of the seed pods which look like a bird's foot when three or four are in a cluster. The red stripe which sometimes appears on the upper petals is thought to act as a guide to the nectar for bees.

Height 10 to 20 cm
Flowering June to October
Other names: Eggs and
*   Bacon*
*   Lady's Slipper*
*   Shoes and*
*   Stockings*
*   Fingers and*
*   Thumbs*
Flower size 10 to 16 mm

Toadflax

This Snapdragon-like plant grows in dry places on banks and roadsides. Its name arises because it looks like flax, although the two are not related. The shape and length of the flower means that only the long-tongued bees can obtain nectar from it.

Height 15 to 50 cm
Flowering June to October
Other names: Brandysnap
Fingers and
Thumbs
Snap Jacks
Flower size 15 to 30 mm

Mallow

Mallow is a very common plant on roadsides and waste land, fields and copses. The fruit that is formed looks rather like a small cake of cheese, which accounts for some of its other names, such as Bread and Cheese, Fairy Cheese or Lady's Cheese.
Both the roots and leaves were at one time used as herbal remedies.

Height 30 to 100 cm
Flowering June to October
Flower size 25 to 40 mm

41

Black Nightshade

Black Nightshade, a weed in gardens and waste places, is also a poisonous plant. Its green or black tomato-like berries remind us that it belongs to the same family as the tomato and potato.

Height 10 to 40 cm
Flowering June to October
Flower size 5 to 10 mm

Ragwort

This common plant grows all summer. Animals do not normally eat it because of its bitter taste when fresh. However, cut Ragwort that has withered does not taste bitter and is eaten by cattle. Unfortunately, it is still

poisonous to them. The plant provides a food source for the cinnabar moth whose caterpillars will often leave nothing but the stem standing.

Height 60 to 130 cm
Flowering June to October
Other name: Stinking Willie
Flower size 15 to 25 mm

Yarrow

Yarrow has feathery leaves and bunches of very small flowers. It has a strong scent and grows in dry meadows, roadsides and on banks. It is related to the Daisy and the Dandelion.

Height 15 to 50 cm
Flowering June to December
Other name: Milfoil
Flower size 2 to 5 mm

Greater Bindweed

The thin-stemmed Bindweed climbs over other plants. The large flowers have no scent. In wet or cloudy weather the flowers close so that the nectar is not spoilt.

Height 100 to 300 cm
Flowering June to October
Other names: Bellbine
*   Convolvulus*
Flower size 60 to 70 mm

Rosebay Willow-herb

Rosebay Willow-herb seeds will keep underground for many years until it is warm and damp enough for them to grow. The plants grow on wasteland and in cleared woodland.

Willow-herb is so called because its leaves resemble those of the willow tree.

Height 60 to 150 cm
Flowering July to September
Other names: French Willow
Fireweed
Flower size 20 to 30 mm

44

Mugwort

Very common on waste ground. The scented-leaved Mugwort has leaves which are silvery on the underside. The Mugwort was once

believed to have magical qualities and to be a protection against witchcraft.

Height 90 to 150 cm
Flowering July to September
Flowering size 3 to 4 mm

Heather

Heather is very common on heaths and moors. Its shallow roots and tough, wiry stems help it to survive in poor thin soils.

The flowers provide a rich source of nectar for bees and the young shoots are eaten by grouse.

Height 7 to 50 cm
Flowering July to September
Other name: Ling
Flower size 3 to 5 mm

Self-Heal

Self-Heal is found by roadsides and on grassy places. It was once used to cure cuts and wounds and sore throats.

Height 15 to 30 cm
Flowering July to September
Other names: Carpenter's
Herb
Hook Heal
Sickle Wort
Prunella
Flower size 10 to 14 mm

Tansy

The Tansy has a spicy scent and very bitter flavour. The flowers are small and like buttons. It grows in waste places by fields and roadsides. At one time it was used in cooking as a flavouring and also as an insect repellent.

Height 30 to 100 cm
Flowering July to September
Flower size 8 to 15 mm

Hawkweed

There are many kinds of Hawkweeds which look like Dandelions. Hawkweeds have several flowers on each stalk.

Height 50 to 120 cm
Flowering July to September
Flower size 20 to 30 mm

Corn Sow-thistle

This large plant which looks like a big dandelion has flowers which open in the morning and close in the afternoon. It grows in arable fields and waste places.

Height 50 to 150 cm
Flowering July to September
Other name: Field Milk
*   Thistle*
Flower size 25 to 50 mm

White Water Lily

Water Lilies grow in still or very slow moving water. Usually the leaves float on the water with the massive stems anchored at the bottom of the pond or stream. The flowers float a few centimetres above the leaves so that the fruit can ripen above the water.

Flowering July to September
Flower size 30 to 60 mm

Harebell

In Scotland the Harebell is known as the Bluebell.
It is found on heaths, hilly pastures and roadsides.
The lower leaves are heart-shaped and have long stalks, but they disappear before the flowers come.
Harebells are not common in Ireland where they are known as Fairybells or Goblin's thimbles.

Height 15 to 50 cm
Flowering July to September
Other names: Bluebell
Windbell
Flower size 8 to 10 mm

Goose Grass

A straggling plant which has hooked hairs on the stem, leaves and fruits.
It clings onto other plants and catches onto passing animals and people.
Goose Grass grows on waste ground, roadsides and hedges.

Height 30 to 120 cm
Flowering May to September
Flower size 1 to 2 mm

Teasel

This prickly stemmed plant grows along paths, roadsides, hedges and on wasteland. In the winter the prickly heads provide food for goldfinches; they are also sometimes used to brush newly-woven woollen cloth. The Teasel is still grown commercially in Somerset for this purpose.

Height 90 to 200 cm
Flowering August to
September
Flower size 30 to 40 mm

INDEX OF BRITISH WILD FLOWERS